Plymouth's Past Through Postcards
Part 1

Guy Fleming
Western Evening Herald

This version of the book is virtually as originally published, presenting the work of Guy Flemming. There are now additional pages at the back providing information about the publisher, Arthur L Clamp.

The republishing project is being managed by Arthur's grandson, Steven Gibson. We aim to find all the research that he was involved in publishing, preserving it for the next generation as part of 'The Clamp Collection'.

An Introduction to the Cards

If it was one of my uncles who forced me to swim by gently lowering me over the side of a rowing boat in Plymouth Sound and muttering cheerfully, "It's up to you now!", it was my grandmother who unconsciously instilled into the enjoyment of collecting postcards.

She sent me my first when I was away from Plymouth at school. It was a sun-saturated view of the Hoe and I've kept it ever since. Others followed, often including terse little notes from various relatives for not writing. I kept those too.

Then nothing happened until the 1960s when I began many years of travelling all around Britain, Belgium and the Netherlands. I bought postcards of many of the places I had to visit, scores of them. In doing so I came across a few fading postcards of Plymouth in its Edwardian grandeur. Old emotions stirred and I was off! I picked my way through card collections at antique shops in such places as Worthing and Southampton (having lived in both) and didn't I get some bargains!

The postcard pursuit continued after I moved back to Plymouth in 1980, and here are some of the results. I hope you enjoy them.

My thanks are due to the ubiquitous Mr. Arthur Clamp for constant supplies of enthusiasm, to my esteemed colleague, Jon Massey, who wrote the captions for Crownhill, to Gerald Barker for general advice and to many others who have helped in one way or another. Oh! by the way, many postcards, or letters too for that matter, used to be delivered on the same day they were posted. And all for ½d or a 1d!

© Guy Fleming,
14 Churchway,
Weston Mill,
Plymouth, Devon

St. Andrew's Street, Plymouth

Recognise the chunky building on the left, taken about 1898? It is now the Merchants House, the largest and finest example left of the mid-sixteenth century style. Three seventeenth century Mayors are known to have lived there. The house was opened to the public in 1978 after restoration by the city council over a period of five years.

Harry Lauder

There's no mistaking the kilted, spatted Harry Lauder on one of his rare visits to Plymouth. The elderly gentleman in the background is the legendary R. J. Fittall, town clerk from 1917-1935. Facing Harry Lauder is Councillor Stanley Leatherby, Mayor of Plymouth in 1933, about the time this snap was taken.

LYMOUTH PROMENADE PIER

View of the Pier
Who could forget the leisured sunlit days sauntering on the old Pier, one of the city's most popular features? Built in 1884, it was a distinctive landmark with its domes, wrought-iron railings and prominent clock. Dances on the Pier invariably were well patronised, and so were the summer shows, the tea parties with a trio trilling in the background—or, just fishing with a line off the end, watching the paddle steamers plough by.

Theatre Royal
The Theatre Royal, opened in 1813, was designed by John Foulston and, together with the adjacent hotel and the adjoining Athenaeum, formed a group which gave Plymouth its character for three-quarters of a century. The Royal could seat 1,192, about the same number as its modern namesake. It closed down in 1936 and after demolition the Corporation sold the site to a cinema combine.

PLYMOUTH. THEATRE ROYAL.

Old Town Street, Plymouth

Old Town Street
The famous Spooners' Corner is just out of view, near end on the left. Drake Circus was first applied to the island block at the far end of this busy thoroughfare in 1905. This survived the war but was demolished to make way for road extensions and a shopping precinct. No picture of this era would be complete without one of those swaying, rattling trams!

Bedford Street

Bedford Street and George Street vied with each other as main shopping areas. This lovely Edwardian shot shows Dingles on the left with John Yeo's (slightly "down-market" perhaps) further down, also on the left. Yeo's wooden floors had grills spaced along them. The compiler remembers being taken there as a child for brown, leather button-up gaiters.

Bedford Street

The towering neo-gothic Prudential Assurance building marked the end of Bedford Street. Opened in 1904, it survived the "blitz", although all surrounding buildings were destroyed. The building's plum-red form could be identified from many parts of the city. It encroached a few metres onto the advancing Armada Way and so was one of several fine buildings removed by the demolition squads.

BEDFORD STREET, PLYMOUTH before the German Air Raids.

MOUTH, BEDFORD STREET FROM ST. ANDREWS CROSS

Guildhall

Bedford Street with its fashionable stores, including Dingle's, Yeo's and Pophams, was destroyed, never to rise again. Quaintly, the directional sign for Torpoint survived. For years the bleak wastes of the old shopping centre seemed to give the lie to the optimistic notices which sprouted, promising: "We shall rebuild here after the war".

George Street
6d. for any article is clearly seen on the building towards the end of this view of George Street and a reminder of Plymouth's newspaper, *The Western Daily Mercury*, which ceased publication in 1921, will also bring back memories.

The livery was maroon and white and the fares were usually 1d. Tram service No. 5, seen here, plied between the Theatre Royal, Friary Station and Prince Rock. The motor bus, built about 1923, had wheels with pneumatic tyres, incorporating better brakes. Then, as now, you paid as you entered! And the wheels have turned full circle as Plymouth's transport undertaking is beginning to operate mini-buses.

St. Andrew's
The intersection of Basket Street and Bedford Street was known as *St. Andrew's Cross* after the memorial which stood within the beautiful railed garden (left). St. Andrew's, most of it dating from the fifteenth century, was a "town" church in a special sense long before the Reformation. The Corporation had provided the material for building the massive square tower and Thomas Yogge, a one-time mayor, dug into his pocket for the labour. It was completed in 1430.

Guildhall, One

The Guildhall was opened in 1874 by the Prince of Wales, later Edward VII. With the municipal buildings across a square, flanked by St. Andrew's tower to the east and, later, a new post office to the west, it made a new focal point as well as becoming the major centre for social events and meetings of every kind.

Guildhall, Two

At 8.39 p.m. on the grey evening of 20th March, 1941, the sirens sounded the death knell of the old city, only two hours after King George VI and Queen Elizabeth had departed following a Royal visit. The full weight of the "blitz" fell and, the following evening, the raiders came back in overwhelming force, 150 of them. The Guildhall was gutted and the municipal offices wrecked; St. Andrew's was left roofless and windowless.

GUILDHALL SQUARE AND ST. ANDREW'S CHURCH, PLYMOUTH

Drake's Circus

Parts of Drake Circus survived the "blitz", becoming a refuge for bombed-out firms like Spooner's (see bottom left and top right). Other businesses located in this area by 1950, when the picture was taken, included Gertrude's wool store; Frank Martin, the watchmaker and John Westcott's, coal merchants.

Plymouth: Westwell Street

Perkins corner was a favourite landmark for the pre-war generation — and the shop offered some good bargains, too, particularly in trilby hats. The Y.M.C.A. is on the opposite corner with the main post office further down the street. The trees — still with us, happily — fringed a cemetery, removed in the 1950s for the extension of Armada Way, amid accusations of "desecration". The operation was carried out stealthily by night.

Canadian Troops on on Plymouth Hoe

The arrival of 25,000 volunteers from Canada on 14th October, 1914, constituted one of the most extraordinary sea processions in history. The armada of 33 liners was not only a secret but a complete surprise to the Plymouth authorities, save for a handful at Admiralty House. It had been destined for Southampton but German submarines were reported to be laying in wait for them and they were immediately diverted to Plymouth. The troops later formed rank on Plymouth Hoe, as seen here. Many of them were to die in battle at Vimy Ridge.

So had these Canadian troops, 25,000 of them — see text next to the centre photograph.

Procession

A procession of local dignitaries winds its way up Lockyer Street for the unveiling of the War Memorial in the summer of 1919. Lady Astor is walking with Sir Arthur Shirley Benn, who represented the Drake division from 1910-1929. The former Town Clerk of Plymouth, Mr. Robert Fittall, walks behind. A robust extrovert, he was quite capable of digging committee chairmen in the ribs and demanding, "How can you be so stupid?" And Lady Astor? She had been elected that year as the first woman M.P. to take her seat in the Commons.

Like the swimming matches and galas for instance. One attraction which will be remembered by many is the subject of the picture below.

Plymouth Swimming Matches

These were great gala occasions, awaited with eager anticipation. The Hoe would be packed with spectators—as here, in 1907—many with relatives who were plunging about and cavorting with varying skills. Swimming was a much more common exercise than now and Plymouth produced a hardy crop of skilled swimmers.

Not, perhaps, what every best-dressed young woman wore around the streets of Plymouth in the early 1930s, but many of them did. Funny how fashion turns full circle though—this coy young damsel would hardly attract a second glance if she walked like this through Plymouth's modern streets!

Plymouth Hoe Bandstand
"Oh, listen to the Band!" And they did, too, in their hundreds. The Hoe bandstand was a prized possession to generations of Plymothians. Sousa's marches would belt out under the cloudless skies—well, sometimes they were!—receiving a ripple of applause from elderly and young alike, mixing in the rows of wooden, tip-up seats. There was great atmosphere induced by those musical heaves and boomps and the crowds loved it.

Post Office
This well-proportioned building was put up in the 1920s and was architecturally acceptable. It stood in Westwell Street at the western end of Guildhall Square which it complemented rather well. The post office was yet another victim of the "blitz". The Matthew's inscription is intriguing, and will bring back memories for some. Restaurants were in the habit of *giving* customers such keep-sakes (or reminders?) with their own names embossed.

St. Budeaux

With its lone parade of shops and sparse residential development, as seen here, St. Budeaux—named after a Breton saint—was a self-contained community until its absorption into Devonport in 1898. It is an ancient place, with parish registers dating back to the fifteenth century. The squat building on the right foreground is the Baptist Chapel opened in 1902 after the congregation had for several years used a room above a stable. It is now a filling station, the Chapel having moved up and around the corner into Fletemoor Road.

St. Budeaux Station

This former London and South Western station opened in 1890 to meet the growing commuter demands into Plymouth. It had a staff of three which coped manfully with a busy schedule, which included many "up" and "down" mainline expresses and a plethora of local services.

Plymouth Girls

This might even have had St. Budeaux for its setting. For the self-contained village was a distinct entity from Plymouth or, for that matter, Devonport too. This card would have been judged just that little bit risqué in 1905.

Plymouth in Mind
A dream of a place? Well certainly the thousands who patronised the ice rink at Millbay thought so!

Millbay Ice Rink
This was a popular skating venue for years even if, sometimes, patrons wore starchy evening dress on top of their skates, as here. It was adjacent to where Telecom House now stands and the admission fee was 2p. Opened before the First World War, it could take several hundred skaters. This is intriguing; the possibility of an ice rink for Plymouth was turned down in 1982.

Friary Station
The old London and South Western Company, formed by a group of Southampton merchants, got its line down to Tavistock and along Tamarside to reach Devonport in 1890. The following year it opened its new Plymouth terminus at Friary, site of a thirteenth century monastery run by the Brothers of Our Lady of Mount Carmel. Later, the Company was absorbed into Southern Railway who used Friary as their terminus for the Plymouth to Waterloo run. It became a goods depot in 1958.

Union Street. Plymouth.

Union Street
If a sailor didn't know his way around Union Street he hardly qualified to be in the Service! Hordes of well-moneyed matelots would spill all over the pavements, literally sometimes, freely spending their pay, often during the first weekend ashore.

Looking West
The road, built by Foulston in 1811 over marshland, continues to magnetise Servicemen, and others, bent on "a good night out". It sprouted many popular rendezvous, such as William's Cafe. The *Carlton*, *Savoy* and *Gaumont* cinemas did brisk business and the Fifty Shilling Tailors lived up to its reputation.

PLYMOUTH. UNION STREET.   83942.

Grand Hotel and R.W. Yacht Club, Plymouth

Grand Hotel and Great Western Yacht Club
After a packed meeting at the Drill Hall in 1889, W. E. Gladstone was almost besieged outside his hotel on the Hoe, with up to 100,000 people clamouring for him. Plymouth journalist R. A. J. Walling remembered how, in acknowledgment, Gladstone stepped on to the balcony of the Grand, "a short, spare figure with a noble head, his silver hair shining in the gas light, his cloak wrapped round him against the night air".

Drakes Reservoir

By a shady nook and a babbling brook, well, some splendid fountains, anyway. And how well they sprayed, high and wide, providing a soothing scenario for those taking a rest on one of the nearby seats in this secluded oasis. The shops on North Hill still stand, with the beautifully proportioned tower of St. Matthias Church fingering its way to the skies on the crest of the hill.

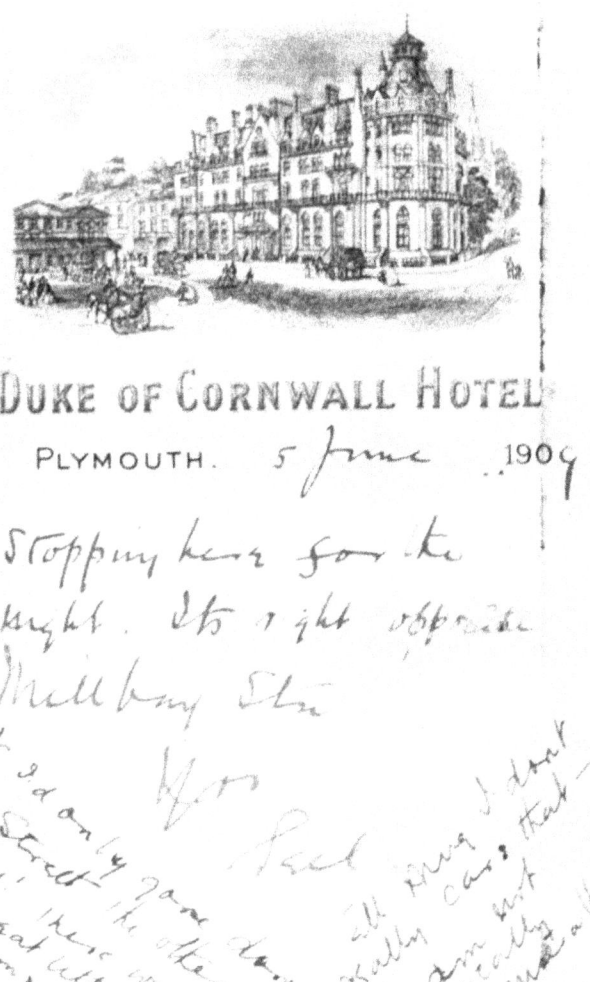

Duke of Cornwall Hotel

The Duke was built in 1865 opposite Millbay Railway station on the site of the *Old Saracen's Head*. The last passenger train pulled out of Millbay in 1941, although goods trains used the line for another thirty years. The Duke retains its air of cloistered good taste. The correspondent on this postcard seems to have had more than his fair share of troubles!

Palace Theatre Interior

Gone but not — surely — forgotten. Most of the 1,900 seats in the Palace were taken out when the old place was transformed into a nightclub in 1984. The Palace opened in 1898 as a music hall which, in essence, it remained for most of its life. The interior was elaborately carved and gilded with painted panels around the dome. Many superb shows were staged at the Palace through the years, some with stars of international repute. But it experienced many vicissitudes and for one unhappy period was a bingo hall. Its final fate was sealed when the new Theatre Royal opened in Royal Parade.

Mount House School

Wolf cubs and scouts played a prominent part in "character building" at the school, which used to be at the end of Hartley Drive but dispersed to Tavistock during the war, never to return to its native hearth. But so did a few good whacks over the backside, as this compiler has rueful cause to remember. Devonport M.P., Dr. David Owen, went to Mount House — did he ever have to "bend over"?

Mount House School, Plymouth *South Front School Group of Boy Scouts*

Personal

It is hard to believe that this tranquil woodland setting in the late 1930s is now covered with tarmacadam for the new A38 trunk road. It used to be ideal picnic country, as the compiler discovered, seen here with his mother and cousin. Widey Wood was a paradise playground for children. We lived in nearby Kneele Gardens, so they were handy for a short jaunt. Not far away was Widey Court, one-time headquarters of King Charles I and Prince Rupert during the Civil War of the 1640s.

Plymouth Market Day.

'Juicy Oranges 2 a Penny.'—'Ted Weekes' Cough-no-more 1d. a packet.'—'I say, who'd have a large Hake for 4d.'—'Boot Laces, 1d. buys another half dozen; half dozen for a 1d.' 'Here you are Mum, a large stick of Tripe for 1½d.'—'Ladies' hair pins, hat pins, safety pins and dangerous pins.'—'Bananas, all ripe, 2 a 1d.—(*Police*: 'Move on with that handcart.') 'Pantomime Song Book a 1d., containing Come home Bill Bailey, There's work in the Dockyard yet, So get your hair cut.'—'Evening Herald' 'Fine fresh Water-cresses.'—'English Violets.' 'Tooth Paste 1d. a box.'—'Tomatos 3d. a lb.' 'I say, here's a beauty, who'll buy a nice young Rabbit for 9d.'—'Sold out Bill?' 'No! I'aint took enough for me lodgings yet.'—'Are we down hearted? No!'—'Let's have a drop of Gin, old dear.'

B.T.

How much for a Meal?

And there *were* free dinners for the unemployed before the First World War too. They received precious little else from public bounty, even though these well-known cries from Plymouth Market, in East Street, do show how cheap it was to eat. Read through the slogans, authentic all of them, and you'll catch something of the animated calls which assaulted shoppers in one of the most popular rendez-vous of old Plymouth.

DAILY ROUTINE
OF A
SOLDIER'S LIFE
AT PLYMOUTH.
Set to Well-known Tunes.

6 a.m.—**Reveille**—"Christians awake, salute the happy morn."
6-45 ,,—**Rouse Parade**—"Art thou weary art thou languid"
7 ,,—**Breakfast**—"Meekly wait and murmur No."
8-15 ,,—**C.O.s Parade**—"When He Cometh."
9-15 ,,—**Manoeuvres**—"Fight the Good Fight."
11-15 ,,—**Swedish Drill**—"Here we suffer grief and pain."
1 p.m.—**Dinner**—"Come ye thankful people come."
2-15 ,,—**Rifle Drill**—"Go labour On."
3-15 ,,—**Lecture by Officer**—"Tell me the Old Old Story"
3-30 ,,—**Dismiss**—"Praise God from Whom all blessings flow." Allelujah!
5 ,,—**Tea**—"What means this anxious eager throng."
6 ,,—**Free for the Night**—"O how thankful we are"
6-30 ,,—**Out of Bounds**—"We may not know, we cannot tell."
10 ,,—**Last Post**—"All are safely gathered in."
10-15 ,,—**Lights Out**—"Peace Perfect Peace."
10-30 ,,—**Inspection of Guard**—"Sleep on, Beloved"

Daily Routine

Apt enough, aren't they? I particularly like, *Tell me the old, old story*, partnering lecture by Officer. And how about, *What means this anxious, eager throng?*—for tea? Evidently, Sankey's song-book was a great favourite among the soldiery of the early 1900s!

Plymouth Parody Songs.

Tune—"BECAUSE I LOVE YOU."

Last night down Union Street I walked, and to a maiden fair I talked,
A distance short with her I strolled, the usual tale of love she told,
She said she wanted to be mine, just then Old Derry struck up nine,
I answered firmly, I decline; these words came then from Caroline:
(*Chorus*)—
You know I loved you, from first I met you, drinking Plymouth Gin, down at that Stonehouse Inn,
When wines you brought me, and rings you bought me; now my heart is yours because I love you.

B.T.

A Parody Song

This is part of a parody song—one of many very popular in Plymouth some 80 years ago. They all carried local connotations and were set to catchy and current tunes. This particular young woman seems to have been an easy conquest, though!

Backs of Postcards

They were exquisitely tinted, bore ½d stamps with Edward VII's square image and usually carried copperplate writing on the "flip" side, often with homely if prosaic little messages from a *Bert* or an *Ethel*.

There's magic in those pre-First World War cards of Plymouth, in the distant days when its northern boundary reached only to Hartley reservoir, and beyond was the untamed wildness of Linketty Lane, surrounded by lush pasturelands.

But the messages on the back were great fun, too. Look at these two for a start. Mrs. R. B. Cook, of Birmingham, was addressed by her doting husband in a style which would bring shrieks of laughter to any typists' pool in the land today; likewise, no modern counterpart of Miss Evans, of Chiswick, would receive a card proudly telling of seeing the biggest battleships in the Navy.

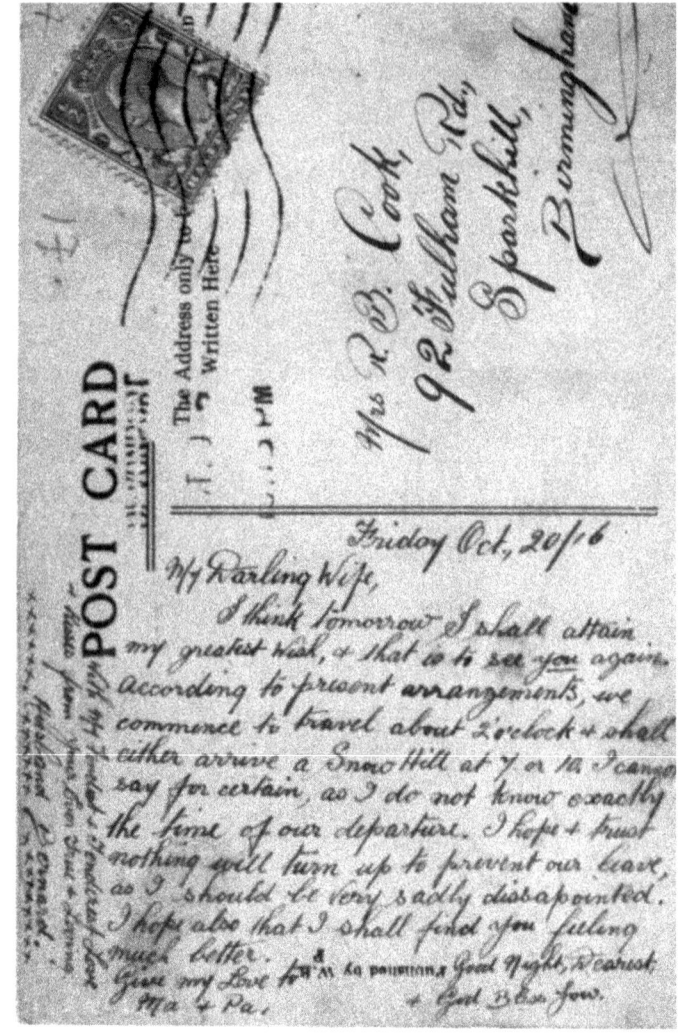

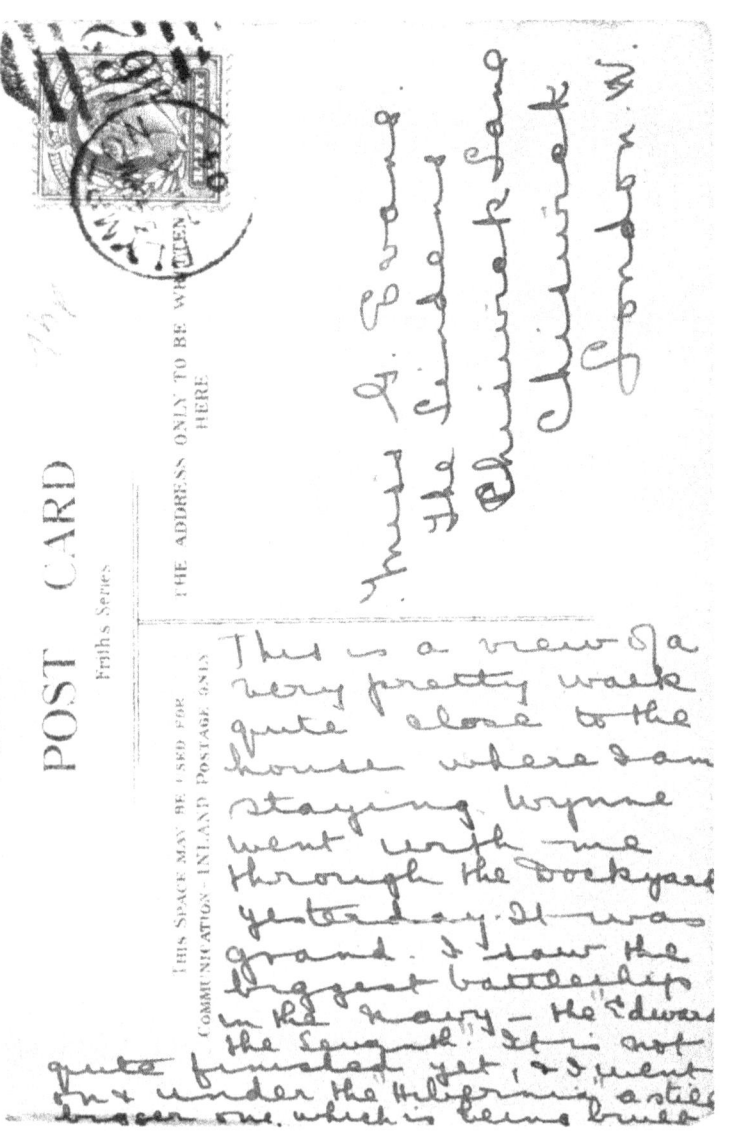

"Not married yet" starkly proclaims a correspondent underneath a shot of the *Hood*, 1890 variety, steaming up the Hamoaze. "After a storm comes a calm", Mrs. K. Flemen of 1, Wolseley Terrace was informed on another. "O.K. I say, you ought to got on", No. 6618 Pte. W. Banks was assured one morning on the back of the "Hairy-Plane" card on page 30.

The back of a "Ye Olde Plymouth Exhibition" card of 1905 contained the stern note, to a Miss J. Morris, of Basingstoke: "I will wait on Devonport Station to meet you. You are over your time, I suppose you know that?" So there!

Well, it all meant something to somebody. In general, people seemed to have more time for each other in those days, and expressed their feelings in a manner which today would seem quaint, even absurd.

Still, how much better it all was than the stilted, "Having a lovely time at Blackpool, wish you were here" type of mini-mouse message that seems to comprise many greatest efforts at communicating feelings these days!

Devonport can be dated from the moment when spades first struck the earth at Point Froward, within today's South Yard. In 1691 the Plymouth analyst James Yonge wrote: "Nothing much happened memorable but that the dock in Hamoaze was begun." He would have been startled indeed could he have foreseen that, barely two centuries later, that same dock would have become the largest naval arsenal in the world, once employing over 20,000 men.

Devonport from Cremyll

The Hamoaze fr Devonport Column

The first houses went up at North Corner; then Fore Street took shape to become the main shopping street until it was wiped away in the 1941 blitz. In 1823 the leading residents of Dock, as the growing dockyard town was called, sent a petition to George IV claiming that they could "no longer be treated as a mere offshoot of the borough of Plymouth; the situation is most anomalous and degrading."

The King took the point and the Home Secretary, Sir Robert Peel, replied to the petition stating that after 1st January, 1824, Dock would be known as *Devonport*. By that time its population had risen to 33,000 compared with Plymouth's 21,000. Still, the town did not evolve into a borough until 1837, electing as its first mayor, Edward St. Aubyn, whose family had owned acres of land for generations.

DOCKYARD GATES AND FORE STREET, DEVONPORT

Fore Street, Devonport

Just up from the Conservative Club on the corner, often used by Leslie Hore-Belisha for twenty years, was the *Tivoli* cinema, just behind the first lamp post. The building almost opposite, next to the *Military Arms*, is now occupied by the *Forum*. Further this way on the right, just past the lamp post in the foreground, stood the 2,000-seater *Electric* cinema, on land now occupied by a garage.

Old Devonport

The signpost points to the Torpoint Ferry and Saltash. A policeman directs what little traffic there is, although the pavements are crowded — they usually were. The former market's majestic tower is all that remains recognisable today. Tozers, left-hand corner, was a Devonport drapery giant. Its owners were prominent in local politics. The lower signpost, pointing to the right, directs traffic to Plymouth!

Fore Street in 1938 shortly before the Forum cinema opened (extreme right), now a bingo hall. Further down this busy street was Hiorns and Miller, the high-class stationers. The post office building, which ran into Chapel Street, was badly scarred in the war, but not destroyed.

Tavistock Street

The *Alhambra Theatre*, which was opened in 1924 by a Colonel Bastard, J.P. (see far right) was first known as the *Empire* and then as the *Metropole*. The theatre's most successful productions were vaudeville. Prices were: Stalls 2/6d, pit 1/3d, circle 2/- and gallery 5d. Bould's huge drapery store is on the immediate right.

Aggie Westons

Agnes Weston set out to create a public house without the drink. She gave the men comfort, bright colours, mirrors and gilding. The cabins could house 900 men and often did. The essential purpose of the Rest has always been evangelistic and there have been some astonishing testimonies to the power of the Gospel through the years. The author served as a Missioner at the former Sailors' Rest, further up Albert Road from the present one, for three years.

Love's Emporium

Jimmy Love's emporium was one of Devonport's "Big Three" stores. The huge shop, specialising in down-market bargains, drew custom from a wide area at the bottom of Catherine Street. Jimmy Love himself was a town "character" serving as a magistrate on the old borough council. His emporium, destroyed in the "blitz", flaunted tall and beautiful roofs, all done in wrought-iron Victoriana.

William Street, Devonport

This popular little thoroughfare stretched from the bottom of New Passage Hill to Navy Row, Albert Road. A fish and chip shop stood on its western corner opposite a pub. There was also a chemist, butchers and a baker on the west side which ended with a little park, thick with trees, which locals knew as *Sparrow Park*. On the other side was a lane which went up to a school. William Street was the main link between vintage Devonport and its newer developments.

Keyham Extension Works (Souvenir of the Royal Visit)

Further tidal and closed basins and graving docks were built, over a period of several years, on the expanse of mud flats at the mouth of Camel's Head Creek. This colossal undertaking involved operations at an exceptional depth behind huge caissons fending off the tides of the Hamoaze. The fully developed schemes were opened by the future King George V and his wife in 1907.

Men Leaving the Dockyard

By 1910 Devonport Dockyard had become the world's largest naval arsenal, with 12,000 employees. The First World War temporarily inflated that figure to nearly 20,000 and in the inter-war years the Yard accounted for a quarter of Plymouth's workforce. Its future seems to be assured, although recent forecasts envisage a slightly reduced workforce.

The Brickfields

Sheep may safely graze—and so they did, right in sight of Devonport Technical College which was opened in 1899. The Brickfields always has been known as the scene for all sorts of sporting events, including boxing tournaments. But it also served as an open-air auditorium for John Wesley who preached there in 1747, defying a menacing mob, and the military, in the process. Unmoved by it all, he spoke for nearly an hour to an attentive throng of several thousand.

Brickfields and Technical School, Devonport

Devonport Market

The tower at the south end of Devonport Market, built in 1852, was a fine specimen of an Italian campanile. The clock tower still stands but within the Yard extension. It had been a familiar landmark. The Market was "magic" to thousands of customers from all over Tamarside who loved its particular atmosphere as well as the well-stocked fish, meat and butter stalls.

THE MARKET, DEVONPORT.

St. Paul's Church, Devonport

The foundation stone for this church was laid in 1847 and the building's architect came from the St. Aubyn family. It seated 400 adults. This picture of Morice Square was taken about 1904 looking up from King Street to Ordnance Street. It was shot from the old Royal Naval and Military Free School, open to the children of Servicemen, Yardies and watermen. It could take up to 600 of them and was immensely popular. The church was another blitz victim.

St Paul's Church.

Training Brigs

Perhaps not red sails in the sunset, but sails—full and whipped by the wind—certainly. It must have made a moving spectacle as the sun gently set on the Sound and the tall, strong ships came majestically up to harbour.

Hamoaze and Dockyards

The Hamoaze has provided one of the most remarkable harbours in the world. Nearly six miles in length, and half a mile across, it is almost completely landlocked, the only approach from the sea being a narrow entrance at Devil's Point through a deep channel some 500 yards across. Most of the land within the dockyard was owned by the St. Aubyn family, from whom it was leased for many years.

Torpoint Ferry

The first Earl of Mount Edgcumbe launched the Torpoint Ferry in 1790 with the help of Reginald Pole Carew, of Antony. By 1794 the Liskeard mail was being carried on the ferry. There is still a great demand for the ferry service, subsidised by the toll charges from the Tamar Bridge, two miles upstream. There has been vague talk of building another bridge near Torpoint, but this seems impracticable given the current financial situation.

Funeral Cortege of Victims

The A8 submarine disaster took place in Plymouth Sound at the start of exercises on the way to Looe. Crowds line the road by Stoke Damerel Church paying their last respects to the lost submariners. Horses and carriages patiently wait in the long procession.

1905 A8 Submarine Disaster

The funeral procession of the ten victims of this disaster are seen here passing along Paradise Road towards Plymouth cemetery on 15th June, 1905. The old station building of the London and South Western Railway is on the left of this scene. Sailors head the large procession carrying wreaths watched by civilians and police with guns held facing downwards.

Inspection on the Hoe

Another kind of parade was this—of volunteers assembling for their annual inspection on the Hoe in 1906. Such an event was as much a social as military occasion, attracting the men's relatives and friends from a wide radius. Of course the Hoe always has been used to this kind of affair, from the days when over 10,000 troops assembled in 1625 prior to Charles I's abortive war against Spain.

Plympton

The Priors of Plympton owned Sutone—later Plymouth—until 1439, when the long-suffering townsfolk threw off an increasingly unwanted stranglehold. Plympton is not only older but was at one time larger and more important than its neighbour by the sea. Plympton R.D.C. administered much of the area now well within the city boundary until 1938.

The castle, remnants of which still stand, its famous grammar school (Sir Joshua Reynolds was a pupil there), and its two large and ancient parish churches gave Plympton a quietly distinguished air which it has never completely lost.

The green and lush open areas seen here have long been seized on by builders to become part of Plymouth's apparently unceasing urban extension. Some Plymptonians still are not reconciled to the boundary extension which swallowed them up in 1967.

Plympton Station

At one time nearly all the long-distance expresses called at Plympton, apart from the sixteen trains a day routed on the rail-motor service from Saltash. The station was opened by the South Devon Railway in 1848 and flourished for many years until the growth of car ownership. Eventually, after faltering unsteadily, the station closed on 2nd March, 1959, with the 7.25 p.m. stopping train from Newton Abbot to Saltash.

Stonehouse from Mount Edgcumbe

Stonehouse

A small community existed at Stonehouse as early as the seventh century. A stone house, with a deer park, gave its name to the district. To the west, and divided from it by the large and marshy salt-water lake of Sourpool, lay the tiny, thriving Sutone.

Stonehouse

King Edward III granted the Stonehouse property to Stephen Durnford in 1368, hence the origin of the more modern street name. In later centuries a mixture of county, naval and Plymouth families gave vent to a considerable social life, with the Durnford Street gentility vying with each other over style of house and number of servants.

TOWN HALL, STONEHOUSE.

The Winter Villa, Stonehouse

Stonehouse

By the mid-1800s, Stonehouse was a cramped buffer state of 20,000 people. It was called *East Stonehouse*. Its western counterpart was on the other side of the water, a hamlet under Mount Edgcumbe, then part of Devon. An urban council was appointed in 1894, with its eastern frontier at the Palace Theatre in Union Street.

R.N. Hospital, Stonehouse

The building began in 1758 on the shores of Stonehouse Creek. When it was completed four years later it had the distinction of being the first hospital in the country to boast of small groups of buildings, effectively isolating the patients from each other. With landing steps down to the water's edge, sick and wounded seamen could be put ashore direct from the boats. The steps, in use until 1919, survive still. The future of the hospital seems assured.

Hooe Lake and Radford Castle

The mock castle-like building stands on the large retaining wall of Radford Lake. Below is the tidal Hooe Lake partly seen here with two small sailing boats moored in front of the castle.

Radford Lake and Woods

Now open to the public, this locality was once part of the grounds of Radford House, home for many years of the Harris family. Today many a Sunday afternoon stroll is enjoyed in this beautiful part of the city.

Drill Hall

With seating for 10,000, the Drill Hall—situated nearly opposite the former Millbay Station—was the largest indoor venue in the West. Yet it was filled every night for four weeks in 1905 by the American evangelist Dr. Reuben A. Torrey and his ebullient song leader, Charles M. Alexander. There were no posts at all in the centre of the Drill Hall and it had the appearance of a long tunnel.

Mr. CHARLES ALEXANDER.

Charles Alexander

Alexander, who introduced "The Glory Song" to Plymouth and was a greatly loved figure, wrote to his wife of one gathering: "We had a number of Cornishmen last night. I got them to stand in testimony and they put fire into the meeting immediately". People began queueing three hours before the meetings began. Incredibly, a few of the converts from those far off days were still alive, and happily testifying, in 1983.

Old Art Gallery

Harris and Sons was one of the large drapery stores in down-town Plymouth at the turn of the century. This card advertised the firm's Christmas gifts—much of it chunky and, to the modern taste, ugly. The picture of a British bulldog with a pipe sticking out of his mouth (end wall, on the right) was found in many a good Tory home. A contemporary antique dealer would be glad to get his hands on some of the articles displayed.

Plym Bridge

This has served as a tranquil rendezvous for generations of Plymouth people. It was outside the Plymouth boundary until 1967. Even now it is sometimes difficult to imagine that a throbbing metropolis is close at hand, except in the rush hour, when it is used as a short cut to the Estover Industrial Estate. But the "maidens fair" in this picture would have known nothing of that!

Plym Bridge near Plymouth.

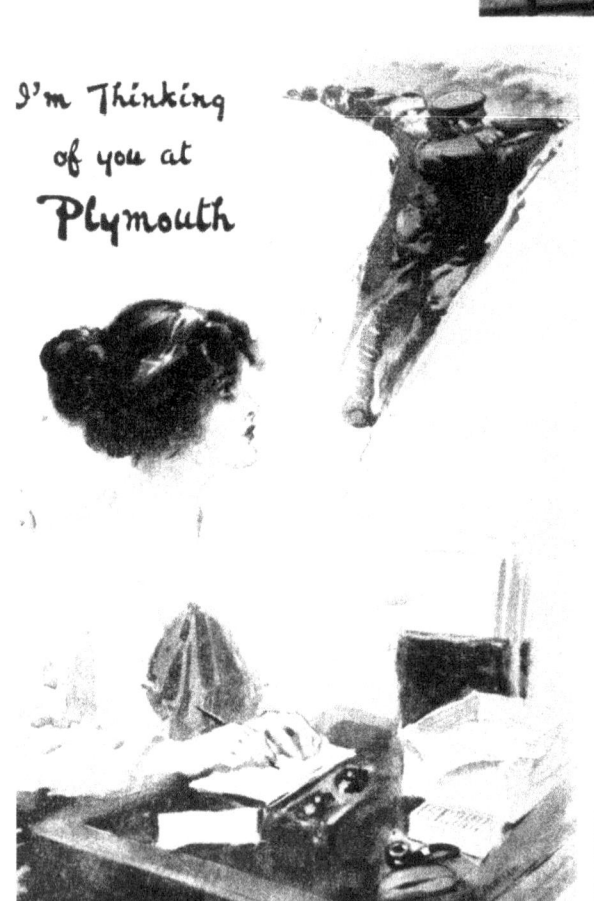

I'm Thinking of You at Plymouth

And so were thousands of other young women in First World War Plymouth. Many lost husbands or sweethearts after that numbing wait for the dreaded, and fearfully long, casualty lists. Every battle in France and Belgium brought one, but none like the Battle of the Bois de Buttes in May, 1918. There the 2nd Devons, made up largely of wartime conscripts, went down to hopeless odds, and scores of Plymouth families were bereaved.

St. Mary's Church, Plymstock

The large fifteenth century tower of the once country parish church of Plymstock is recorded here around the year 1900. The parish hall, on the left, was built in 1901 and the buildings on the right still remain much as they are viewed here. There was, of course, no traffic on the road in those days, only children who could play safely on the roads and lanes without fear of being knocked down.

CHURCH ROAD, PLYMSTOCK

The Moths
Typical of the groups which entertained Pier patrons were *The Moths*, a well-known pre-1914 troupe of versatile actors and singers, and the *Komikal Skots Komedy* group. They were in demand throughout the area and were great favourites at Devonport Park.

The Komikal Skots Komedy Kompany, Victoria Park, Devonport, 1910.

Victoria Park Show in 1910
The old Stonehouse creek was filled in to form Victoria Park many years ago and the area has been used for countless entertainments from fêtes to meetings and sports events. This early card recalls part of one entertainment for the local folk in 1910.

At Rest on the Guildhall!
So his spatted feet kicks his bowler into the air. Of course, the face of this jolly Johnny, apparently clutching on to the Guildhall tower, was reproduced on similar cards of towns all over Britain. He must have been quite a guy!

Widey Farm

A vignette from the past and the not so-distant past at that. This was part of the early Widey Court lands, and the farm was worked until 1937. Officers from Crownhill Barracks lodged there sometimes, and its cattle often were to be seen on grazing land now covered by houses.

Raglan Barracks

All a mistake this, at least, the buildings were. They were earmarked for India but the *Men from the Ministry* made one of their muddled mix-ups and they were erected in Devonport, sun resistant flat roofs, verandahs and all. The Indian soldiery in Cawnpore had to contend with Raglan's intended buildings and they weren't very pleased about it either. The parade ground was a huge attraction for local people who enjoyed seeing the massed companies of soldiers marching to the beat of gaudily-attired bands. The Barracks were built in the 1850s and demolished in 1969.

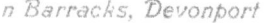

Three Crownhill Bygones

Those were the days, my friend, they thought would never end — until the sixties' road-builders buried all but the tiniest traces of these tranquil scenes under a sea of ugly grey concrete. The elegant tinted postcard shows the village of Crownhill before the First World War — and nothing the bowlered gent was reading in his newspaper could have inspired as much shock and horror as the columns upon columns of compulsory purchase orders published in the Evening Herald in 1968. Only two building in this scene remain today, the now-modified Methodist Church in the foreground, and the end-terraced house next to it. Everything else was pulled down in one of the most massive demolition exercises in Plymouth since the "blitz", including the Crownhill Barracks, out of view behind the fence on the right. One householder held out against the demolitionists and as a result, 5 Crownhill Road is the only remnant of the terrace of houses and shops seen here. Today, the white-elephantine Crownhill flyover cuts deep through the middle of the former terrace, the road is a busy dual carriageway, and the gent, should he stand there today, would probably be overcome by traffic fumes.

Plymouth Girls
This galaxy of girls (were they local?) was common enough on greetings postcards in the early 1900s. The man on the moon seems to be regarding Smeaton's Tower with delight—of course, they would have seen a lot of each other.

1905 Postcard
This delightful card carries local views inside each figure in the date, a common ploy on postcards in those far-off days.

Devonport Panorama
Multi-view postcards were very popular at one time, and still are, to an extent. This one gathers together some of Devonport's most noteworthy landmarks, familiar indeed to all who lived in the old borough town. The shot of Fore Street could indicate that a naval vessel had recently docked.

Arthur L. Clamp – the man behind the books

Arthur Leslie Clamp was a man of boundless energy with a passion for helping others, particularly through his love of history. A printer by trade, he started his career in a printing company before moving his family from Exeter to Plymouth to teach at the Plymouth College of Art and Design, where he eventually became the Head of the Printing Department.

Arthur with his five children.

A Devoted Family Man

Despite his love of teaching, Arthur prioritised his family, always making it home by 5:30pm for tea. He and his wife, Rosemary, raised five children: Susan, Angela, Elizabeth, David, and Steven. Arthur would often combine his love of family and history by taking his children on Sunday walks, encouraging them to appreciate historical monuments by taking photos or making crayon rubbings of gravestones for his books. The family home at 203 Elburton Road was a hub of activity, with a large garden, featuring a two-storey fort and a makeshift swimming pool.

A Lifelong Learner and Adventurer

Arthur's thirst for knowledge extended beyond history to a deep curiosity about the world. He was passionate about exploring different cultures, traditions, and cuisines, often taking advantage of his long summer holidays as a teacher to travel to places like India, Russia, South America, the middle east and the USA, sometimes bringing one of his children along. This adventurous spirit even influenced his home life, as seen by the short-lived family tradition of steam-cooking vegetables after a trip to Iceland.

History is a prominent feature of family days out

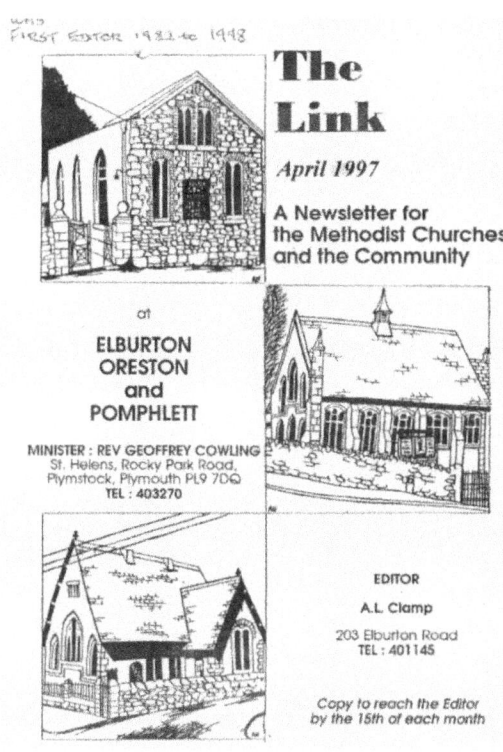

Community and Philanthropic Spirit

His commitment to serving others was evident in his long-standing involvement with the Elburton Methodist Church. He was the Sunday School Superintendent for over 15 years and served as the editor of the wider church's monthly newsletter, "The Link," for a similar duration. After Rosemary's very sad passing, Arthur later remarried and, following a chance encounter with a professor from India, established a connection with a missionary school in Chennai. Together with his new wife, Christine, he co-founded a "Sponsor a Child's Education" program that continues to this day.

Pictured left – The cover of 'The Link' complete with hand drawn sketches of each church by Angela
Below right – Arthur Clamp promoting his latest book
Below left – Arthur at home with his first wife, Rosemary
Below centre – Arthur on holiday with his second wife, Christine

A Legacy of Learning and Positivity

Arthur's greatest passion was history, which he brought to life through tireless research, documentation, and the many books he authored. He was driven by a need to "never be stuck in a rut," constantly seeking new experiences, meeting new people, and expanding his knowledge. With a positive attitude and a great sense of humour, he was always ready to help others, leaving a lasting impact on his family and community. His children, Susan, Angela, Elizabeth, David, and Steven, remember him with love and gratitude.

David Clamp, 2025

A Legacy of Local History

Below is the story of how Arthur L Clamp began writing books, in his own words, drafted shortly before he passed away in 2001. I have only made minor alterations to this text, correcting grammatical errors that he did not survive to correct himself. When I first discovered this text, I was shocked to see my name mentioned. It seems that, unbeknownst to me, I shared my first PC with him. I suspect he used it during the day when I was at school, although I do have one memory of sitting with him and showing him how it worked. It has been a pleasure to pick up where he left off and see his books republished and redistributed, and to know that I was part of the story, even back then. It was also fascinating to discover that his pricing structure matches the way I have tried to price the books, with a third going to local sellers and the rest covering printing costs with a little left over for my expenses.

I am his eldest grandson, and it is a privilege to curate his legacy, which we are calling 'The Clamp Collection'. The very last line of the text originally reads "The following pages list all the titles." Sadly, that page is missing and we have no record of all the books he published and knowing that some of those were researched by other authors makes the process of finding them even harder. I look forward to one day completing the collection and seeing them all available again. And maybe, one day, I'll even start writing my own to add to the series. For now, here is his story in his own words.

Steven Gibson, 2025

Writing and Publishing Booklets on Local Topics and Areas

I started this interest in either 1968 or 1969 when living in Woodford. I had by these dates established the Department of Printing and I think I must have been looking for something different to do. The first titles were of A5 size proofed from type set at Clarke, Doble and Brendon, Ltd., Plymouth printers, and then made up into pages and printed at Sawtell and Neilson, Ltd., Totnes.

Then began a slow process of getting them out to shops, etc. which proved to be more time consuming and difficult than actually researching, writing and getting the books into print. However, I persisted and opened a business account with Barclays Bank on the Broadway. I was advised to give it a title so I called it "Westway Publications". There came along another problem, one of storage of paper and finished books which was solved when the family moved to Elburton in 1970.

I changed the printer to Penwell, Ltd., Callington, Cornwall, as he was then just setting up himself and his prices seemed very reasonable. I did not get any of the printers to make up the complete books. I hand folded the flat printed sheets, stitched the books on a small manual table stitcher and trimmed them in a small hand turned guillotine which I bought from someone in Penzance for £40. It was brought up in a van.

The trouble and time going to and fro to Callington was too much so I transferred the printing to PDS Printers, Prince Rock, Plymouth, and I have been with them ever since. Now they are at Plympton which is easy to reach and they fold the flat sheets which was turning out to be a long chore which only saved a small part of the printing costs.

All my first titles were written by myself. I took the photographs and developed them in the loft of the house, the type was set by now on a computer situated in the house at Elburton from which I had collected photographic lengths of text to cut up and law down as pages.

At some point I decided that I would do my own film processing of lith film so I bought a large second hand process camera from Kingsbridge and learnt through trial and error to make line negatives of the text and halftone negatives of the illustrations which proved more difficult than I anticipated. The main problem was trying to keep the developer in the large dish at the correct temperature as any change would affect the developing time. I replaced this old camera with a brand new one bought from Croydon, Surrey, costing £900. This has turned out to be a great asset cutting out an expensive part of the printer's costs and one crucial aspect of the work which I could control.

By the middle 1970s there were many outlets I had contacted in Plymouth, up to Dartmoor, Exeter, around to Torbay, Totnes, Dartmouth and the South Hams. The market for local books was much greater than I had first thought and through getting to know many local people undertaking research themselves had the chance to help and make up books for other people who had in most instances, got together a collection of photographs with some text in a rather muddled way. Through my experience in print I was able to shape up their work and get it into print and in every case I had to pay the printer and let the person have the royalties. In the majority of titles produced in this manner this was another way of producing titles and it did give some profit to my work. However, I must say that in a few cases I lost out by either the other person getting the numbers wrong, not returning any monies from stock I delivered or they thought that more of their books should have been sold.

The print run was usually 1,000 copies and from time to time I have had reprints of 250 copies. It took about ten years to clear the first print run so I always had large stocks in the garage, workshop, etc. The numbers sold during the early years was about 7,000 copies a year increasing to around 9,000 copies and for the whole of the enterprise about 500,000 have been sold. The booklets have become part of the local scene and many people collect them, shops regularly order copies and I go around certain areas month by month restocking or replacing titles as necessary.

During the past year or so I have started setting the text on a Packard Bell PC, something which I should have done some years back. I share it with Steven Gibson, my grandson. There appears to be no end to the market for local books, but I could not earn a regular income because of the long time it takes to sell stock.

However, now exceeding 100 titles made up mainly of A4 twenty-four page booklets, some folded guides, with selling prices set with a third going to the shop which is the trade custom, the original idea has been quite successful and could go on for ever.

Apart from monetary benefits, however spasmodically these might be, I have learnt a lot myself, met many interesting people and have become part of the local scene with requests to give talks and to advise people about getting into print.

Arthur L Clamp, 2001

This newspaper article, published by the Evening Herald on 17th August 2001, forms a good record of his life. Just as he encourages us to learn more about local history, we encourage you to learn a little about him. For that reason, we have included these pages at the back of all the most recently republished books, in honour of his memory and recognition of his contribution to the community.

www.ingramcontent.com/pod-product-compliance
Lightning Source LLC
Chambersburg PA
CBHW061404070526
44584CB00031B/4161